American Lives

William Penn

Jennifer Blizin Gillis

Heinemann Library
Chicago, Illinois

Designed by Heinemann Library
Photo research by Jill Birschbach
Printed and bound in China by WKT Company
Limited

09 08 07 06 05
10 9 8 7 6 5 4 3 2 1

Library of Congress Cataloging-in-Publication Data
Gillis, Jennifer Blizin, 1950-
  William Penn / Jennifer Blizin Gillis.
    v. cm. -- (American lives)
  Includes bibliographical references and index.
  Contents: No hope at home -- Childhood -- Early
years -- A rebel -- A true quaker -- An outlaw --
More jail time -- Joy and sadness -- Holy experiment
-- A colony begins -- Pennsylvania -- Troubled times -
- The experiment ends.
  ISBN 1-4034-5963-0 (HC), 1-4034-5971-1 (Pbk.)
  1. Penn, William, 1644-1718--Juvenile literature.
2. Pioneers--Pennsylvania--Biography--Juvenile
literature. 3. Quakers--Pennsylvania--Biography--
Juvenile literature. 4. Pennsylvania--History--
Colonial period, ca. 1600-1775--Juvenile literature.
[1. Penn, William, 1644-1718. 2. Pioneers. 3.
Quakers. 4. Pennsylvania--History--Colonial period,
ca. 1600-1775.] I. Title. II. Series: American lives
(Heinemann Library (Firm))
  F152.2.G55 2004
  974.8'02'092--dc22

                    2003027789

Acknowledgments
The author and publishers are grateful to the
following for permission to reproduce copyright
material:

Cover photograph by Bettmann/Corbis

Title page, pp. 5, 6, 9, 13, 20, 22, 23, 25, 26, 29
Bettmann/Corbis; pp. 4, 12, 16 Corbis; p. 7 Courtesy
of Historical Society of Pennsylvania Collection/The
Bridgeman Art Library; p. 8 Victoria and Albert
Museum, London/Art Resource; p. 10 Mike
Reed/Eye Ubiquitous/Corbis; pp. 11, 19 Archivo
Iconografico, S. A./Corbis; pp. 14, 18 Mary Evans
Picture Library; p. 15 Stock Montage; p. 17 Profiles
in History/Corbis; p. 24 Francis G. Mayer/Corbis; p.
27 Historical Society of Pennsylvania; p. 28 Atwater
Kent Museum of Philadelphia/The Bridgeman Art
Library

The publisher would like to thank Michelle Rimsa
for her comments in the preparation of this book.

Every effort has been made to contact copyright
holders of any material reproduced in this book.
Any omissions will be rectified in subsequent
printings if notice is given to the publisher.

For more information about the image of William Penn
that appears on the cover of this book, turn to page 5.

Contents

Some words are shown in bold, **like this.** You can find out what they mean by looking in the glossary.

No Hope at Home

In 1680, life was not good for **Quakers** in England. They were often thrown in jail, whipped, or worse. Why? There were many reasons. They would not take off their hats, even for a king. They treated everyone as equals, even women. They did not believe the government should run churches. Quakers believed in living simply and peacefully. The government did not trust them.

William Penn was a Quaker from a wealthy family. He had spent most of his money getting other Quakers out of jail. He had written many **tracts** explaining the Quaker religion.

This painting shows William receiving the **charter** for Pennsylvania from King Charles II. It gave him land between the colonies of Maryland and New York.

4

Only one picture of William was painted while he was alive. This picture shows how an artist thought William might have looked as he got older.

William tried to tell the government that Quakers did not want to make trouble. It was no use. The government would never leave the Quakers alone.

Then, William remembered some money his father had lent the king. The king had never paid it back! William asked the king for land in the New World instead of money. Now, he could start a **colony** where Quakers could worship as they wanted and take part in the government.

Childhood

William was born in London, England on October 14, 1644. He had one brother and one sister. His mother came from a wealthy family.

William's father was the captain of a ship. He was often away at sea. He was friends with King Charles I. He made sure everyone knew he was loyal to the king. This way, he could have a good job and live in a good neighborhood.

William's father was also named William. He wanted his son to be friends with whoever was in charge of the government, so that he would have an easy life.

The Life of William Penn

1644	1657	1662	1667	1672
Born October 14	Hears a Quaker speaker in Ireland	Leaves Oxford University	Arrested for first time for Quaker beliefs	Marries Gulielma Springett

War in England

*William was born during a **civil war**. In those days, a person's religion was very important. Before the war, only people who belonged to the **Church of England** could live in certain neighborhoods or have government jobs. After the war, the new government made it against the law to belong to the Church of England.*

When William was three years old, he got **smallpox.** It made him lose most of his hair. For the rest of his life, he wore wigs most of the time.

William had this picture of himself painted when he was 22. It is the only picture that was painted during his lifetime. At that time, he wanted to be a soldier. That is why he is shown wearing **armor.**

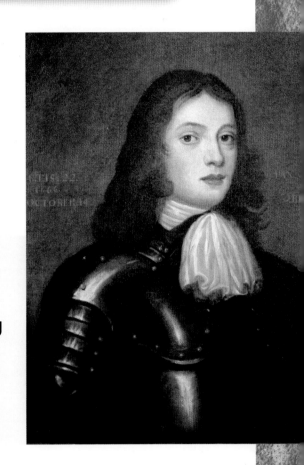

1681	1692	1694	1696	1712	1718
Receives **charter** *for* **colony** *from King Charles*	*William's charter is taken away*	*Gulielma dies; William gets Pennsylvania back*	*Marries Hannah Callowhill*	*William has his first stroke*	*Dies on July 30*

7

Early Years

The group that won the **civil war** was called the Roundheads. They killed King Charles I. Their leader took over the government. Instead of being killed or thrown in prison like many of the king's friends, William's father was put in charge of some ships. His ships won a battle, so the Roundheads gave him land and a castle in Ireland. But his luck did not last. He soon lost a sea battle and the Roundheads sent him to prison, too.

William learned to read and write at home. When he was eleven years old, he went to Chigwell Free Grammar School. Other boys there got into trouble for playing tricks or sneaking out, but William liked to study.

The Roundheads put King Charles I to death for **treason** in 1649.

A man named George Fox started the Society of Friends, or Quakers. He said his followers should tremble, or quake, when they heard the word of God.

When William's father got out of prison, he moved his family to their castle in Ireland. William's father was interested in other religions. In 1657, he invited a **Quaker** named Thomas Loe to visit. William became interested in the Quaker religion.

Good Student

William studied Greek, math, and writing. He had a good memory and was a good writer. He also spent many hours alone each day reading the Bible.

A Rebel

William was almost fourteen when the leader of the Roundheads died. William's father went back to England to help Charles II become king of England again. King Charles II then made him a knight and asked him to be in charge of some English ships.

William's father sent him to Oxford University in 1660. Oxford students had to go to services in the **Church of England.** They had to wear special robes to show that they were learning to be leaders in the church.

When he was sixteen years old, William went to Christ Church College at Oxford University. Young men from wealthy families were sent there so they could later get good jobs in the government.

While in France, William took classes at Saumur Protestant School. There he learned about respecting other religions and being peaceful at all times.

William began to visit a teacher who spoke against the church. He began refusing to go to church services or wear the robes. In 1662, William was sent away from Oxford because of his behavior.

William's father was angry with him. He sent William to visit France, so he could learn to be a gentleman. William came back to London in 1664 and studied law.

A True Quaker

Under King Charles II, the **Church of England** was the official religion again. It was against the law to be a **Quaker.** At this time, William's father sent him to Ireland to take care of the family castle and land.

William began going to Quaker meetings in Ireland. In 1667, a soldier began disturbing a meeting where William was worshiping. William threw the soldier out. Soon, more soldiers came and arrested everyone there.

Anyone was allowed to speak during a Quaker meeting, even women. Most people in the 1600s thought women should not speak in public.

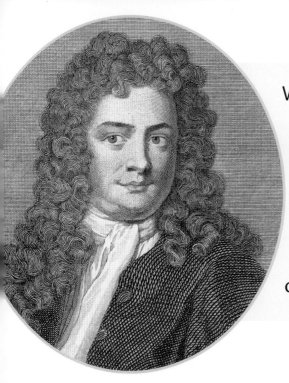

William had learned to dress and act like a gentleman in France. With his long, curly wig, lace sleeves, and sword he looked out of place among the Quakers in their simple, dark clothes.

The mayor sent all the Quakers to jail. He was surprised to see a gentleman like William with a scruffy crowd of Quakers. He told William to go home. But William refused and went to jail with his friends. At that moment, he knew he would be a true Quaker for the rest of his life.

Laws for Quakers

In those days, it was against the law for more than five Quakers to be in the same place at one time. Quakers who broke these laws could be put in jail or whipped in a public place.

An Outlaw

In jail, William wrote a letter explaining why he and the other **Quakers** should be freed. It worked! William and his friends were freed.

William went back to England. He traveled and spoke at Quaker meetings. At one meeting, he met Gulielma Springett. Her parents were Quakers. He and Gulielma decided that they would marry one day.

This image shows a typical Quaker meeting in England in the 1600s.

William began writing many **tracts.** He wanted to help people understand what Quakers believed. In 1668 the **bishop** of London said that one of William's tracts was against the law and against God. William was sent to jail in the Tower of London.

After nine months, a **chaplain** visited William. William explained that the bishop had misunderstood his writings. The chaplain told William to write another tract that explained exactly what he meant. In 1669, William wrote a new tract and was freed.

William's life in the Tower of London was very hard. In winter, it was freezing cold. In summer, it was hot as an oven.

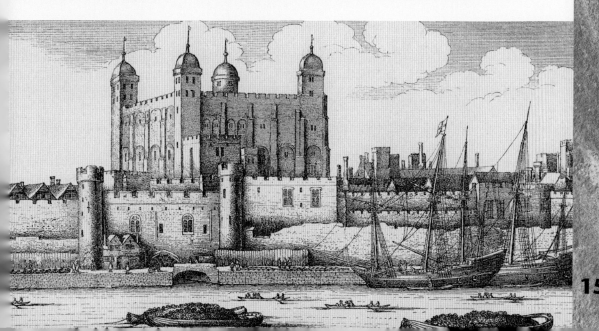

More Jail Time

William's father sent him back to Ireland to keep him out of trouble. William found out that many Irish **Quakers** were in jail. He hired a helper named Philip Ford. They divided their time between taking care of the Penn lands and helping Irish Quakers.

William wrote letters to people in government. He asked them to free the Quakers. By June 1670, William had gotten all Irish Quakers out of jail. He went back to England and began to preach Quaker teachings in the street. He was arrested and sent to Newgate Prison.

Newgate prison was one of the worst prisons in England. Many prisoners there died of diseases.

William used his time in Newgate Prison to write more **tracts.**

William's father was very sick. He was afraid he might die before he saw his son again. He secretly paid for William to be freed from prison. William arrived home just before his father died on September 16, 1670.

A Change in the Law

*A **jury** at William's trial found him not guilty. But the judge did not like their decision. He ordered the jury to be put in jail until they said William was guilty! Because of William's case, English law was changed so that a judge could not change a jury's decision in a trial. It later became an important part of law in the United States.*

Joy and Sadness

This illustration shows a couple being married by a priest in the 1600s.

On April 4, 1672, William Penn married Gulielma Springett. Nine months later, Gulielma had a baby girl, who soon died. In 1674, Gulielma had twins—a boy named William and a girl named Mary. Baby William soon died but in 1675, Gulielma had another boy named Springett. Not long after Springett was born, Mary died. In 1678, Gulielma had another girl named Letitia. Another son, also named William, was born around 1680.

Penn's father had left him a lot of money. And Penn had his family's land in Ireland, too. Philip Ford, Penn's helper, came to England. Penn put Ford in charge of his money.

Penn wrote more **tracts.** He begged the government not to mistreat people who did not worship in the **Church of England.** But nothing worked. Finally, Penn asked King Charles II for land in North America.

Penn wrote many tracts in his lifetime. Many were about the freedom to follow any religion a person chose. He also traveled to preach in the Netherlands and Germany.

Holy Experiment

In 1681, King Charles II gave Penn a **charter** for a **colony** in North America. He said it must be called "Penn's Sylvania," or Penn's woods, to honor William Penn's father.

Penn was in charge of the whole colony. He could set up the government any way he wanted. He owned everything on and under the land. He just had to pay the king some beaver skins, gold, and silver every year.

King Charles II (1630–1685) was the ruler of Great Britain and Ireland.

Pennsylvania

The king gave Penn land that lay between Maryland and New York. Many Native Americans lived there at that time.

It was a good deal for Penn, and an even better deal for the king. He hoped the **Quakers** would move to Pennsylvania and stop causing trouble in England.

Penn called Pennsylvania a "holy **experiment.**" He wanted to show that people could make their own laws, run their own government, and live together in peace. He began to write advertisements so people would buy land and move to the new colony.

A Colony Begins

Penn started writing the Frame of Government to explain how the **colony** would work. Penn would choose a governor, but the colonists would vote for other lawmakers. People would be free to worship any way they chose. Every child over twelve years old would learn a **trade.**

Penn wrote to the Native Americans in Pennsylvania. He wanted to buy land from them instead of just taking it away. He planned a capital city called "Philadelphia." Penn wanted it to have wide streets.

PENNSYLVANIA: A PRIMER.

The FRAME of the
GOVERNMENT
OF THE
Province of Pennſilvania
IN
AMERICA:
Together with certain
LAWS
Agreed upon in England
BY THE
GOVERNOUR
AND
Divers FREE-MEN of the aforeſaid
PROVINCE.

To be further Explained and Confirmed there by the firſt *Provincial Council* and *General Aſſembly* that ſhall be held, if they ſee meet.

Printed in the Year MDCLXXXII.
FAC-SIMILE OF TITLE PAGE OF PENN'S "FRAME OF GOVERNMENT, 1682."

Penn's *Frame of Government* was changed many times, but it was a good plan. Pennsylvania's state laws are based on Penn's writings.

Travel to Pennsylvania

Penn wrote in his advertisements that the trip to Pennsylvania from England would cost 5 pounds, 10 shillings for adults, or about $176 in today's money. A trip for a child would cost 50 shillings, or about $17 today. Babies could travel for free.

The first **settlers** left England for Pennsylvania in 1681. Penn put his cousin in charge of the colony until he and his family could get there. But when Penn was ready to sail for Pennsylvania, his wife Gulielma was **pregnant** and could not travel. Penn had to go to his new colony alone.

There were about 700 European **settlers** in southern Pennsylvania before Penn started his colony. People from Sweden, Holland, and Finland lived in houses like these along the Delaware River.

Pennsylvania

In October 1682, Penn's ship landed in New Castle, Pennsylvania. Penn visited Philadelphia. Then, he sailed up the Delaware River to visit his new house.

Penn spent a lot of time with the Susquehannock and Delaware (also called Lenni Lenape) tribes in Pennsylvania. He visited their villages, ate their food, and even learned to speak their languages. Penn treated Native Americans with respect, so they never attacked **Quaker settlers** in Pennsylvania.

This painting shows William Penn (left) signing a treaty with the Native Americans.

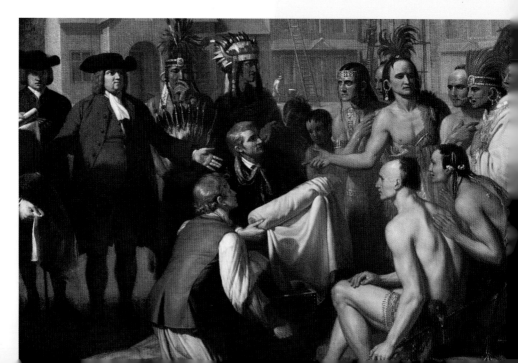

William Penn's house was called Pennsbury Manor. He did not spend much time there, because he only lived in Pennsylvania for a few years.

Penn made nine different treaties, or peace agreements, with the Native Americans. In October of 1683, he bought the land at the mouth of the Susquehanna River from the Susquehannocks.

But Lord Baltimore, who owned the **colony** of Maryland, said it was part of his land. Lord Baltimore went to England to complain to the king. In 1684, Penn sailed to England to speak for his colony.

Big Changes

Soon after Penn arrived in England, Charles II's brother James became king. But Charles's daughter Mary wanted to be queen. James was forced to leave the country. Penn had been friends with James, so Mary and her husband William said Penn was a traitor. They took Pennsylvania away from him in 1692.

Gulielma got sick and died in 1694. Soon after, Mary and William gave Pennsylvania back to Penn. Then, Penn met a **Quaker** named Hannah Callowhill. They were married in 1696.

In 1692, Queen Mary and King William took Pennsylvania away from Penn. Penn lost all of his money because he could not collect rent from colonists.

In March 1696, Penn married Hannah Callowhill in Bristol, England.

In 1699, after being away for sixteen years, Penn decided to move back to Pennsylvania. Then he got some bad news. He had once put Philip Ford in charge of all his money. Now Philip said Penn owed him more than 10,000 pounds—about $409,000 in today's money. Philip made Penn sign a paper making Philip the owner of Pennsylvania.

Hannah and William Penn had a son, John, in 1700. He was the first in the Penn family to be born in Pennsylvania. They had a second son, Thomas, in 1702. They had their first daughter, Hannah Margarita, in 1703. They had other children in later years, named Margaret, Richard, Dennis, and Hannah.

A Sad Ending

In 1701, Penn got more bad news. The English government wanted to take over the **colonies.** Penn went to England to speak against that. He was so poor that he had to sell some land to pay for his trip.

Penn learned that Philip Ford had died. Philip's wife said Penn would have to pay her the 11,000 pounds he still owed Philip. In 1708 Penn was sent to **debtor's prison** because he was too poor to pay.

Today, this statue of Penn stands on top of the Philadelphia City Hall. This old photo shows how large the statue is.

Penn was buried next to his first wife, Gulielma, and some of their children in this graveyard in England.

Penn's friends learned that Philip Ford had been cheating Penn for many years. They paid Philip's wife some money to get Pennsylvania back for Penn. They also got him out of debtor's prison.

In October 1712, Penn had a **stroke.** In 1713 he had another stroke. After that, his mind wandered and he did not recognize people he once knew. Penn died on July 30, 1718.

A Family Treasure

*Pennsylvania belonged to the Penn family until it became a state at the end of the **Revolutionary War.***

Glossary

armor   metal suit worn by soldiers to protect them from swords and arrows

bishop   leader within the Church of England

chaplain   member of a group that assists a bishop

charter   document from the government that gives certain rights to a person or group of people

Church of England   Christian religion has the king of England as its highest leader, rather than the pope, and is the official church of the nation

civil war   war between people who live in the same country

colony   group of people who move to another land but are still ruled by the country they moved from. People who live in a colony are called colonists.

debtors' prison   jail for people who owed money

experiment   test to see if something will work

jury   group of people who make decisions in a court of law

pregnant   carrying a child

Quaker   person who is a member of the Society of Friends, a Christian religion that says every person has an inner light and their own way of believing in God

Revolutionary War   war from 1775 to 1783 in which North American colonists won their independence from Great Britain

settler   person who makes a new home in a new place

smallpox   disease caused by a virus that makes skin blister and is often fatal

stroke   sudden illness that is caused by a problem in the brain and that can leave people unable to move or speak

tract booklet that contains religious writing

trade job that involves making something, such as printing, baking, candlemaking, and so on

treason act of going against one's country or its government

More Books to Read

Kroll, Steven. *William Penn*. New York: Holiday House, 2000.

Stefoff, Rebecca. *William Penn*. Philadelphia: Chelsea House, 1998.

Places to Visit

Pennsbury Manor
400 Pennsbury Memorial Road
Morrisville, PA 19067
Visitor Information: (215) 946-0400

Arch Street Friends Meeting House
320 Arch Street
Philadelphia, PA
Visitor Information: (215) 627-2667

Index